# Beyond the Shadows: Unlocking the Mystery of Bigfoot

Edward Turner

Published by Oliver Lancaster, 2023.

# Also by Edward Turner

Ghosts of Paris: Ten Haunted Places in the City of Love
Appalachian Nightmares: The Top 10 Creepy Creatures of the Mountains
Asia's Top Ten Cryptids: Legends, Sightings, and Theories
Beyond the Shadows: Unlocking the Mystery of Bigfoot
Evil Women in History: Uncovering the Gruesome Crimes of Ten Notorious Female Killers
Ghosts of London: Ten Haunted Places in The City
Ghosts of New York: Ten Haunted Places in The Big Apple
Ghosts of Oregon: The Top 10 Haunted Places You Must Visit
Missouri Nightmares: The Top 10 Chilling Legends
Mothman Unleashed: Into the Darkened Skies
North America's Top Ten Cryptids: Legends, Sightings, and Theories
Philly's Phantom Encounters: Exploring the City's Most Haunted Places
Secrets of the Deep: The Mystery of the Loch Ness Monster
Unsolved Mysteries: Delving into the Shadows of Infamous Murders and Enigmatic Killers
Unveiling the Shadows: A Journey into Financial Crimes and Scandals

# Beyond the Shadows: Unlocking the Mystery of Bigfoot

# BEYOND THE SHADOWS: UNLOCKING THE MYSTERY OF BIGFOOT

# BEYOND THE SHADOWS: UNLOCKING THE MYSTERY OF BIGFOOT

# Prologue: Into the Unknown

The world is filled with mysteries, some more intriguing than others. The Loch Ness Monster, the Bermuda Triangle, UFOs—these have all fueled mankind's fascination with the unknown. However, one enigma stands at the forefront of human curiosity: Bigfoot, the elusive creature of the North American forests. This creature, despite hundreds of sightings and tales recounted over generations, remains hidden, shrouded in shadows, lurking just beyond our reach and understanding. But why? What makes Bigfoot so elusive, so mysterious?

To answer these questions, we need to venture deep into the unknown, unravelling layers of mythology, folklore, scientific research, and eyewitness accounts. This isn't just about discovering an elusive creature; it's about understanding our fascination with the unknown, our innate desire to explore the unexplored, and our quest for knowledge beyond the fringes of our current understanding.

Let us begin our journey in the dense and wild forests of North America. Imagine being enveloped by thick fog, the crisp forest air filling your lungs, and the occasional rustle of leaves, teasing the presence of the unseen. The only guide in this undulating sea of green is the occasional shaft of sunlight piercing through the canopy. It is here that we begin our quest, here in these depths, where the shadows hold secrets—secrets that have inspired awe, fear, and wonder for centuries.

The mystery of Bigfoot is as deep and labyrinthine as these forests. It's an enigma that reaches into the very heart of human nature, our curiosity, and our insatiable need for answers. The creature we call Bigfoot, Sasquatch, or the Yeti has evoked these primal feelings in generations of people. And it's this exploration of humanity's collective curiosity and fascination with Bigfoot that this book aims to unravel.

What is it about Bigfoot that makes us question our understanding of the world? What is it about this creature that scares us, yet draws us closer? Why, despite hundreds of years of advancements in science and technology, have we been unable to conclusively prove or disprove its existence?

This book, "Beyond the Shadows: Unlocking the Mystery of Bigfoot", is not just about the creature itself. It's about the people who have dedicated their lives to seeking it, the cultures that have woven it into their folklore, and the scientists who have risked their credibility in the pursuit of the truth. It's about the dichotomy between belief and scepticism, and the thin line that often separates the two. It's about humanity's timeless fascination with the unexplainable, the indefinable, and the unknowable.

So, dear reader, I invite you to join me on this journey. Prepare to suspend your disbelief, to entertain the extraordinary, and to venture into the world of the unexplained. Our guide on this journey is the elusive, intriguing, and enigmatic Bigfoot. Let us step beyond the shadows and unlock the mystery that is Bigfoot.

# Chapter 1: Legends in the Wilderness

———

## 1.1 In the Footprints of Folklore

The tale of Bigfoot is not confined to modern times. Its roots are deeply entrenched in the lore of different cultures worldwide, transcending borders and generations. From the Native American tribes who first inhabited the land to stories from far-off continents echoing strikingly similar narratives, Bigfoot is a story of global folklore.

Native American folklore is rich with tales of large, hairy, humanoid creatures living in the woods. Different tribes referred to them by different names, but many of their descriptions eerily match our contemporary understanding of Bigfoot. The Salish tribe of the Pacific Northwest, for instance, spoke of Sasquatch, a word that translates to "wild man" or "hairy man." The Choctaw told tales of the 'Kashehotapolo', creatures covered in long, shaggy hair, and having a terrible odour. For these cultures, these beings were as real and relevant as the other animals in the forest.

Notably, these creatures were not mere figments of fancy; they held a significant place in the tribes' spiritual and cultural fabric. They were often seen as intermediaries between the human and spiritual realms, symbols of nature's raw power, or as warnings to respect the wilderness and its mysteries.

While the prominence of Bigfoot is most prominent in North American cultures, its narrative is echoed across the globe, showing striking parallels that cannot be ignored. In the icy heights of the Himalayas, the local Sherpas speak of the 'Yeti,' a large, bipedal creature with a striking resemblance to Bigfoot. The indigenous Australians have tales of the 'Yowie', a creature that shares the same description—a large, hairy, humanoid creature living in the wild. Even in Scandinavia, there are tales of 'Trolls', giant, hairy creatures living in the most remote corners of the wilderness.

These stories, spread across different cultures and continents, separated by vast oceans and mountains, suggest a narrative that extends beyond mere coincidence. How could cultures, disconnected by geography and time, weave tales so eerily similar unless there was a kernel of truth to them?

Exploring these tales also takes us into the realm of ancient myths and legends. Ancient Greek mythology speaks of creatures like the Satyrs, beings with human upper bodies and goat-like lower bodies, living in forests and mountains. The Epic of Gilgamesh, one of the oldest known works of literature, tells a story of Enkidu, a wild man raised by animals in the wilderness before being civilised.

These tales and myths, spread across cultures and through the ages, reveal our collective fascination with humanoid creatures that exist on the boundary of civilization and wilderness, human and animal, known and unknown. They reflect our deep-seated need to understand and personify the wilderness and its mysteries, a testament to the enduring allure of Bigfoot.

In essence, Bigfoot's roots run deep, not only through the dense forests it purportedly inhabits but through the annals of human history and culture. It stands as a symbol—a symbol of the wild, the unknown, and the enigmatic. It represents our innate curiosity, our quest for knowledge, and our fear and awe of the unknown.

## 1.2 Tracing the Footprints – Early Encounters and Sightings

BEFORE THE ADVENT OF the internet, before sensational TV shows, and before the viral nature of modern media, there were quiet whispers, stories told around campfires, and hushed conversations about encounters with a creature unlike any other. These are the early documented sightings of Bigfoot, lending a certain degree of credibility to an otherwise elusive narrative.

One of the earliest recorded accounts of a creature akin to Bigfoot can be traced back to the journals of the famous explorers, Lewis and Clark. During their epic journey across the North American continent in the early 19th century, they mentioned encounters with Native American tribes who spoke of 'large, hairy men' living in the wilderness. They also noted mysterious footprints and unusual sounds, although they never claimed to have seen such a creature themselves.

A major turning point came in 1924 with an incident famously known as the "Battle of Ape Canyon". Fred Beck and four other miners were prospecting in the area near Mount St. Helens in Washington state. They reported being attacked by several 'ape-like' creatures, who hurled rocks at their cabin throughout the night. The incident was widely reported in the local press and is often hailed as the moment when the legend of Bigfoot began to emerge from the shadows of folklore into the light of popular culture.

In the ensuing years, several more accounts of Bigfoot encounters trickled into public consciousness. In 1958, a series of large, mysterious footprints found at a construction site in Bluff Creek, California, catapulted Bigfoot into national awareness. The tracks were discovered by Gerald Crew, a construction worker, and were reported in the Humboldt Times, a local newspaper. The footprint cast made from this sighting is one of the most iconic pieces of Bigfoot evidence to date.

Newspaper reports played a significant role in documenting and disseminating these accounts, thus cementing Bigfoot's status in popular culture. In 1967, the Patterson-Gimlin film came to light, arguably the most famous and controversial piece of Bigfoot evidence. Shot in Bluff Creek, California, the short film appears to show a Bigfoot striding through a clearing, glancing towards the camera before disappearing into the woods. The film ignited a firestorm of debate and fascination that continues to this day.

These early sightings and accounts, despite varying in details and circumstances, have a common thread – the encounter with something unexplained, something that defies our understanding of the natural world. They also mark the transition of Bigfoot from the realm of indigenous folklore and into the lens of popular culture and scientific curiosity.

While these reports do not conclusively prove the existence of Bigfoot, they undoubtedly form an intriguing pattern of encounters. They represent a call to explore the uncharted territories of our understanding, to push the boundaries of our knowledge, and to question the limits of our belief.

# 1.3 Cryptid Cousins - Legends Across the World

BIGFOOT, ALTHOUGH THE most renowned, is not the only large, bipedal, hairy creature whispered about in hushed tones or celebrated in legends and folklore worldwide. Similar cryptids, often described with strikingly similar characteristics, emerge from the rich tapestry of cultures across the globe. The Himalayan Yeti, the Australian Yowie, and the Central Asian Almas are just a few of these intriguing counterparts.

Let's journey to the Himalayas first, the roof of the world. Amid the harsh and inhospitable peaks shrouded in snow and mystery, local Sherpas tell tales of the 'Yeti,' also known as the 'Abominable Snowman.' Descriptions of the Yeti echo those of Bigfoot: a large, bipedal creature covered in hair. Sightings, footprints in the snow, and local lore about the Yeti have been a part of Himalayan culture for centuries. Despite numerous expeditions, the existence of the Yeti remains as elusive and enigmatic as the mountains themselves.

Next, we traverse the globe to the vast landscapes of Australia, where the indigenous population narrates tales of the 'Yowie.' Like Bigfoot, the Yowie is described as a large, hairy, and ape-like creature, often standing taller than an average human. The

Yowie's tales are rooted in Aboriginal mythology and continue to be reported in modern times, adding another fascinating chapter in the global cryptid narrative.

Central Asia, known for its rugged mountains and vast steppes, brings us the legend of the 'Almas.' The Almas, according to Mongolian and Kazakh folklore, are wild men, smaller in stature than Bigfoot but nonetheless similarly described as bipedal, hairy, and uncannily human-like. Accounts of Almas have been reported for centuries, with some suggesting that the Almas might represent a surviving population of Neanderthals or another hominid species.

These tales, though originating from disparate cultures and geographical regions, share a common theme: the existence of a large, hairy, human-like creature living in the wilderness, elusive and beyond our complete understanding. The similarities among these cryptids challenge us to contemplate whether they might represent isolated pockets of an undiscovered species or if they are manifestations of a collective unconscious—a primal fear or fascination with something that is both like us and yet not us, something that blurs the boundary between humans and the rest of the animal kingdom.

Investigating these legends also shines a light on our cultural diversities and similarities, revealing how different societies respond to and interpret the unknown. The folklore and legends surrounding these creatures offer profound insights into our shared human condition—the innate curiosity and the desire to explore the unexplained and unexplored.

# Chapter 2: In Search of the Wild Giant

---

## 2.1 The Pioneers – Trailblazers of Bigfoot Research

As the lore of Bigfoot seeped into the public consciousness, it piqued the interest of a handful of intrepid researchers. These pioneers, fueled by a mixture of curiosity, fascination, and the desire to uncover the truth, ventured into uncharted territories and laid the groundwork for modern Bigfoot research. Three names stand out in this context: Ivan T. Sanderson, John Green, and René Dahinden.

Ivan T. Sanderson, a biologist and a prolific writer, was among the first to investigate the Bigfoot phenomenon seriously. His fascination with unknown creatures, or cryptids, led him to establish the Society for the Investigation of the Unexplained, an organisation dedicated to investigating phenomena ignored by mainstream science. Sanderson's extensive field research and his scientific approach to the Bigfoot enigma lent much-needed credibility to the subject. His book, "Abominable Snowmen: Legend Come to Life," was a seminal work on the subject and was among the first to treat Bigfoot and similar entities as potential undiscovered species rather than mere myths.

John Green, a Canadian journalist, was another pivotal figure in the early Bigfoot research community. Known as the chronicler of the Sasquatch, he spent decades investigating sightings, collecting data, and interviewing witnesses. Green's approach was meticulous and systematic. His newspaper background served him well in collating and reporting on Bigfoot sightings, culminating in several influential books, including "Sasquatch: The Apes Among Us." His extensive database of sightings remains one of the most comprehensive resources for Bigfoot researchers.

René Dahinden, a Swiss-Canadian Bigfoot researcher, was known for his relentless pursuit of the truth about Bigfoot. Dahinden spent much of his life dedicated to field research, often living out of a trailer as he travelled across North America following up on Bigfoot sightings and reports. His dedication and passion for the subject made him a central figure in the Bigfoot community. Although he never wrote a book, Dahinden contributed significantly to others' works and was instrumental in getting the Patterson-Gimlin film scientifically analysed.

These pioneers, each with their unique approach and contributions, shaped the early field of Bigfoot research. Their dedication, often in the face of ridicule and scepticism, paved the way for future generations of researchers. They epitomised the spirit of exploration and the pursuit of understanding the unknown, lending a certain credibility to the study of Bigfoot and its enigmatic existence.

By studying these early researchers, we gain insights into the early days of Bigfoot research, a period marked by fascination, exploration, and a growing acceptance of the possibility that there might be more to the world than what meets the eye.

# 2.2 On the Trail – Notable Expeditions and Investigations

THROUGHOUT THE DECADES, the elusive nature of Bigfoot has spurred numerous expeditions and investigations, each aimed at shedding light on this cryptid's enigmatic existence. The pursuit of credible evidence has led to some remarkable ventures, including the Patterson-Gimlin film, the Freeman footage, and the ambitious Operation Endurance.

The Patterson-Gimlin film remains the most iconic piece of purported Bigfoot evidence. Captured in October 1967 in Bluff Creek, California, this minute-long film shows a large, bipedal, hairy creature walking along the creek bed. Roger Patterson and Robert Gimlin, the men behind the footage, claimed to have stumbled upon the creature during a horseback ride. The film has sparked heated debates among scientists, researchers, and enthusiasts alike. Despite various analyses over the years, some claiming it's a hoax and others defending its authenticity, the Patterson-Gimlin film remains inconclusive but undeniably fascinating.

Another intriguing piece of evidence is the Freeman footage, captured by Paul Freeman, a Bigfoot enthusiast, in 1994 in the Blue Mountains of Washington State. The video appears to show a large, bipedal creature moving in the distance, followed by shots of large footprints in the ground. Freeman, a former U.S. Forest Service worker, had reported multiple Bigfoot sightings throughout his life. Like the Patterson-Gimlin film, the Freeman footage has been the subject of scrutiny and debate. Though sceptics point to inconsistencies in the video, it continues to be a significant piece of potential Bigfoot evidence.

Beyond these individual efforts, larger, organised expeditions have also sought to uncover evidence of Bigfoot. Among them, Operation Endurance stands out for its scale and determination. Launched in 2008 by the Bigfoot Field Researchers Organization (BFRO), the operation aimed to gather indisputable evidence of Bigfoot's existence. The multi-week expedition involved dozens of researchers and volunteers scouring the forests of the Pacific Northwest, employing an array of equipment, including night vision scopes, thermal imagers, and sophisticated audio recorders. Although the operation did not produce the conclusive evidence it sought, it did generate a number of potential sightings, sounds, and footprints, contributing to the mounting body of intriguing, though not definitive, Bigfoot data.

These expeditions and investigations underscore the persistent fascination with Bigfoot and the enduring quest to validate its existence. They represent a testament to our collective curiosity, the thirst for discovery, and the enduring allure of the unknown.

## 2.3 Tech on the Trail – Advancements in Technology Aiding Bigfoot Research

AS WE HAVE VENTURED deeper into the 21st century, the pursuit of Bigfoot has been transformed and amplified by significant advancements in technology. From night vision equipment to drones, trail cameras, and advanced audio recording devices, modern technology has opened new doors and provided fresh perspectives in the quest for this elusive creature.

Night vision equipment, for one, has been a game-changer. The ability to penetrate the veil of darkness has given researchers the upper hand in a field where their subject is reputed to be nocturnal. Infrared and thermal imaging cameras allow them to detect heat signatures and movements in pitch-black conditions, lending an edge to nighttime explorations and investigations.

Trail cameras have also proven to be valuable tools in the arsenal of Bigfoot researchers. These motion-activated cameras can be left in strategic locations for days or even weeks at a time, silently capturing images of anything that moves within their field of view. While these devices have yet to capture definitive evidence of Bigfoot, they have contributed to a better understanding of the fauna in supposed Bigfoot habitats and have occasionally captured intriguing images that defy easy explanation.

The advent of drone technology has added an exciting dimension to Bigfoot research. Drones allow for extensive coverage of challenging terrains, hovering over dense forests and scaling steep mountains with ease. They can capture high-resolution images and videos from vantage points that were previously inaccessible. Researchers can now survey vast expanses of wilderness for signs of Bigfoot, all from the safety and convenience of a remote location.

Finally, modern audio recording devices have lent an ear to the wilderness like never before. High-sensitivity microphones capable of picking up faint sounds from a considerable distance have added an auditory dimension to the research. They have recorded numerous unexplained sounds and vocalisations that some believe might be Bigfoot's calls. Such devices have also been used to analyse the famous purported Bigfoot recordings, like the Sierra Sounds, adding a layer of potential acoustic evidence to the mix.

These technological advancements have undoubtedly revolutionised Bigfoot research, equipping enthusiasts and researchers with the tools to probe deeper and more efficiently into the heart of the mystery. While the existence of Bigfoot remains unproven, these technologies continue to enhance our understanding of the wilderness and the potential creatures that inhabit it.

# Chapter 3: Bigfoot Encounters: Tales from the Witnesses

## 3.1 Face to Face – Gripping Accounts of Close Encounters

In the realm of Bigfoot research, witness accounts form the backbone of the evidence. Among the multitude of stories and sightings, certain experiences stand out—instances where individuals had intense, up-close encounters with the elusive creature. These accounts, often punctuated with physical confrontations, eerie vocalisations, and profound psychological impacts, add a personal and visceral dimension to the Bigfoot narrative.

One account that still sends chills down the spine of those who hear it is that of Albert Ostman. In 1924, Ostman, a Canadian prospector, claimed to have been abducted by a Sasquatch while sleeping in his camp in British Columbia. He reported being carried in his sleeping bag across the country before being released in a hidden valley, home to a family of four Sasquatch creatures. Ostman spent nearly a week observing these creatures before making his escape. His detailed description of the creatures and their behaviour remains one of the most striking accounts of a close encounter with Bigfoot.

A more recent incident, reported by a hunter in Washington State in the late 1980s, highlights the potential for physical confrontation. The hunter claimed that while tracking deer, he came across a large, hairy, bipedal creature. When the creature saw him, it reportedly reacted with a loud, piercing scream and advanced towards him. The hunter fired a warning shot, which seemed to deter the creature. This encounter underscores the element of fear and shock witnesses often experience during these encounters.

Vocalizations often play a significant role in close encounters with Bigfoot. Numerous witnesses have reported hearing eerie screams, howls, or grunts during their encounters. One hiker in Oregon recounted an experience where she heard a series of chilling, mournful howls echoing through the forest. She then saw a large figure moving swiftly among the trees. Although she couldn't identify the creature, she was certain that the vocalisations were unlike any wildlife she knew.

The psychological impact of these encounters can be substantial and enduring. Witnesses often report feeling a mix of awe, fear, curiosity, and sometimes trauma after their encounters. Some express a newfound respect for the wilderness and its mysteries, while others grapple with the challenge of having their worldview shaken.

These close encounters, whether chilling or awe-inspiring, serve to deepen the mystery and allure of Bigfoot. They provide a tantalising glimpse into the potential reality of this cryptid, while also highlighting the profound effect such an encounter can have on an individual.

# 3.2 Shared Encounters – When Sightings

# Multiply

ONE OF THE MOST COMPELLING categories within Bigfoot sightings is those incidents corroborated by multiple witnesses. These shared experiences, often involving family encounters, group expeditions, and community sightings, provide a higher level of credibility, given the independent yet matching testimonies. They add a layer of intrigue and persuasiveness to the Bigfoot narrative, challenging the notion that all sightings can be chalked up to misidentification or fabrication.

Consider the family camping trip that turned unforgettable in the summer of 1981 in the Sierra Nevada mountains. The Davis family, consisting of parents and three children, reported an encounter with a large, bipedal, hairy creature near their campsite one evening. The creature reportedly displayed curiosity, watching them from a distance. Although the encounter was unsettling, all family members independently described the creature similarly, reinforcing the consistency of their experience.

Group expeditions also occasionally stumble upon unexpected encounters. A notable incident occurred in 1997 during a BFRO expedition in Skookum Meadows, Washington State. Multiple participants reported seeing a large figure moving through the trees late at night and hearing unusual vocalisations. The following day, the team discovered a large body imprint in a muddy patch, known as the Skookum Cast, which many believe was left by a Sasquatch.

Community sightings, where multiple people from a community or town report sightings within a similar timeframe, add another level of intrigue. The town of Fouke, Arkansas, offers a notable example. In the early 1970s, several residents reported encounters with a creature that came to be known as the Fouke Monster, leading to a local frenzy and inspiring the cult classic film "The Legend of Boggy Creek." The similarity of descriptions among the different witnesses painted a convincing portrait of an unknown creature inhabiting the local area.

Cases of multiple witnesses offer an intriguing lens through which to examine Bigfoot sightings. They underscore the social impact of such encounters, influencing not just individuals but entire communities, and contribute to the ongoing debate about the existence of this cryptid. While scepticism remains in the scientific community, these corroborated accounts continue to fuel the mystery and fascination surrounding Bigfoot.

## 3.3 Under the Lens – Witness Testimonies Through the Eyes of Experts

WITNESS TESTIMONIES form the bedrock of Bigfoot research, providing a vast and varied pool of data. Yet, they also present a significant challenge: how do we evaluate their credibility? In the quest to understand these accounts, psychologists and forensic experts have emerged as crucial players, bringing their expertise to bear on issues of trauma and memory, credibility assessment, and the psychological impact on witnesses.

# BEYOND THE SHADOWS: UNLOCKING THE MYSTERY OF BIGFOOT

The interplay of trauma and memory is a key aspect of many Bigfoot encounters. When a witness reports a Bigfoot sighting, it's often a shocking and distressing event, triggering a surge of adrenaline. This response can affect the memory of the incident, sometimes enhancing recall of certain details while potentially distorting others. Psychologists, with their deep understanding of memory processing under stress, provide valuable insights into how to interpret these reports.

Forensic experts bring their skills in credibility assessment to the table. Using techniques like Statement Validity Assessment (SVA) or Criteria-Based Content Analysis (CBCA), they examine witness testimonies for consistency, coherence, and the presence of specific details that are generally associated with authentic memories. While these techniques can't confirm the existence of Bigfoot, they can help separate potentially credible accounts from those that are likely fabrications or mistaken identifications.

The psychological impact on witnesses is another area of interest for psychologists. Bigfoot encounters can have profound effects, often leading to fear, fascination, and sometimes obsessional behaviour. Some witnesses may struggle with anxiety or post-traumatic stress, while others might find themselves drawn into the world of Bigfoot research, seeking answers to their experience. These reactions add a human dimension to Bigfoot encounters, revealing how they reverberate far beyond the moment of sighting.

In many ways, the analysis of witness testimonies by psychologists and forensic experts represents a fusion of the human sciences with the enigma of cryptozoology. It not only enhances our understanding of the accounts but also provides a deeper look into the human side of the Bigfoot phenomenon. The testimonies, examined under this expert lens, become more than just stories - they become a window into how we respond when confronted with the mysterious and unexplained.

# Chapter 4: The Science of Sasquatch

## 4.1 In Their Footsteps – Examining Bigfoot Footprints and Physical Evidence

One of the most fascinating aspects of Bigfoot research lies in the analysis of footprints and other physical evidence. Track casts, dermal ridge analysis, and studies into size and morphology all provide tangible artefacts around which researchers can focus their scientific investigations.

Bigfoot footprints are among the most commonly reported physical evidence. These impressions, often found in remote woodland areas, tend to measure between 15 and 24 inches in length, vastly larger than any human footprint. Track casts made from these footprints serve as a physical record, offering researchers the opportunity to study them in detail. For example, renowned researcher Dr. Jeff Meldrum has amassed a collection of over 300 track casts from across North America, which he studies for patterns and consistency.

A critical aspect of footprint analysis is the examination of dermal ridges, akin to human fingerprints. Some Bigfoot tracks show intricate patterns of dermal ridges, suggesting the presence of a living creature rather than a simple hoax. In the 1980s, forensic expert Jimmy Chilcutt made headlines when he claimed to have identified unique dermal ridge patterns in some Bigfoot track casts, separate from those of any known primate species.

Although these findings are debated, they add a fascinating angle to the study of Bigfoot tracks.

The size and morphology of the footprints offer additional clues. Bigfoot tracks display certain unique features, such as a lack of a pronounced arch and a flexibility in the foot's mid-section, more akin to non-human primates than to modern humans. These morphological details challenge simplistic explanations, suggesting that if these tracks are hoaxes, they are remarkably sophisticated ones.

Other physical evidence, while less common, also plays a significant role. Reports of hair samples, for instance, have led to some intriguing, though inconclusive, results. Meanwhile, anecdotal evidence of damage to vegetation, structures, or animal populations can provide contextual support to other forms of evidence.

Despite the compelling nature of this physical evidence, none of it has yet provided definitive proof of Bigfoot's existence. Critics argue that footprints can be convincingly faked, and other physical evidence often lacks the rigorous chain of custody needed for scientific validity. Nevertheless, this tangible evidence forms a central pillar of Bigfoot research, driving ongoing investigations and continuing to fuel debates in this enigmatic field.

## 4.2 Strands of Mystery – The Scientific Examination of Bigfoot Hair Samples

IN THE QUEST TO UNEARTH the truth about Bigfoot, one form of evidence holds a particular allure for its potential to yield incontrovertible proof: hair samples. With advances in genetic analysis, particularly DNA sequencing and mitochondrial analysis, hair samples attributed to Bigfoot have come under rigorous scientific scrutiny, with results that are intriguing, if not yet conclusive.

Hair samples, usually discovered at locations of reported Bigfoot sightings or in close proximity to footprints, provide researchers with an opportunity to probe the mystery at a molecular level. DNA, the blueprint of life, can reveal a wealth of information about the species, gender, and even the individual traits of the creature from which the hair originates.

The process of DNA sequencing involves extracting DNA from the hair follicle and decoding its genetic information. In the case of purported Bigfoot hair samples, researchers aim to identify sequences that do not match any known species, which could suggest an unknown creature such as Bigfoot. However, so far, DNA analysis has typically resulted in matches with known animals, often local wildlife, or has been inconclusive due to degradation or contamination of the samples.

Mitochondrial analysis offers a complementary approach. Mitochondria, the energy factories of cells, contain their own DNA (mtDNA), which is passed down along the maternal line and mutates at a relatively predictable rate. This makes it ideal for tracking species lineage and evolution. Analysis of mtDNA from suspected Bigfoot hair samples can provide insights into the species history of the creature in question. Still, as with nuclear DNA, no definitive proof of Bigfoot has yet emerged from these analyses.

Scientists also compare the physical characteristics of the hair samples with hair from known species. They examine the colour, thickness, length, and microscopic structure. While there have been several instances where the hair didn't match any known species but looked primate-like, these results remain subject to debate.

The scientific examination of Bigfoot hair samples epitomises the intersection of cryptozoology and mainstream science. Despite the inconclusive nature of the results to date, the process underscores the seriousness with which some researchers approach the subject, applying rigorous methods in the hope of uncovering solid evidence. The promise of what these hair samples might eventually reveal keeps the flame of curiosity alight, illuminating the ongoing search for Bigfoot.

# 4.3 Echoes in the Forest – Deciphering Bigfoot Vocalizations

WITHIN THE BODY OF evidence supporting the existence of Bigfoot, audio recordings of purported vocalisations present an intriguing frontier. These often haunting and enigmatic sounds—whether they be howls, growls, or even alleged spoken language—have been subjected to rigorous analysis, with spectrograms, linguistic analysis, and comparisons with primate vocalisations forming key strategies in the pursuit of understanding.

The analysis of Bigfoot vocalisations often begins with spectrograms. A spectrogram is a visual representation of the spectrum of frequencies in a sound or other signal as they vary with time. In the context of Bigfoot research, these are invaluable in visually representing the structure and patterns within a recorded sound. Researchers can compare the spectrogram of a suspected Bigfoot vocalisation to those of known animals to see if it matches any existing species. Several such analyses have resulted in vocalisations that, intriguingly, don't seem to fit any known North American wildlife.

Linguistic analysis offers another angle of investigation, particularly for recordings suggesting complex vocalisations or possible language. The infamous "Sierra Sounds," recorded in the Sierra Nevada Mountains in the 1970s by Ron Morehead and Alan Berry, have been subjected to this type of analysis. Morehead asserts that the sounds represent a complex language spoken by a family of Bigfoot creatures. While the claim is controversial, some researchers, including R. Scott Nelson, a retired U.S. Navy crypto-linguist, support the theory, suggesting the sounds exhibit language-like features.

Comparisons with primate vocalisations provide a further line of inquiry. Given that Bigfoot is often theorised to be a kind of primate, it's natural to compare recorded vocalisations with those of known primates. This comparison helps identify similarities in sound structures and patterns. While some interesting parallels have been drawn, no definitive links have been established.

The analysis of Bigfoot vocalisations underscores the breadth and depth of the research into this elusive creature. Every howl echoing through the forest, every strange chatter captured on audio, fuels the ongoing quest to understand just what kind of creature might be out there. These sounds, filled with mystery and awe, provide yet another piece to the puzzle, adding another layer to the captivating enigma of Bigfoot.

# 4.4 Shadows of Heat – Thermal Imaging in the Search for Bigfoot

IN THE ONGOING QUEST to capture incontrovertible evidence of Bigfoot, technology plays a crucial role, and one of the most exciting developments in recent years is the use of thermal imaging. Through the lens of Forward Looking Infrared (FLIR) cameras, heat signature analysis, and intensive field studies, researchers are opening up the nighttime wilderness, shedding light on the elusive creature that might be hiding in the darkness.

FLIR cameras, originally developed for military use, detect infrared radiation, or heat, emitted by objects. As living creatures emit heat, they stand out against cooler backgrounds, making thermal imaging a powerful tool in wildlife detection, especially in low-light conditions or dense vegetation. These cameras have been adopted by Bigfoot researchers as a way to uncover potential evidence of the creature under conditions where standard cameras would fail.

# BEYOND THE SHADOWS: UNLOCKING THE MYSTERY OF BIGFOOT

Heat signature analysis forms the backbone of thermal imaging research. By examining the heat signatures captured on thermal cameras, researchers can make informed judgments about the type and size of the creature detected. While it can be challenging to distinguish a Bigfoot from other large mammals based on heat alone, unusual bipedal movement or extraordinary size might point to something out of the ordinary.

Field studies employing thermal imaging cameras have led to some intriguing footage. For example, the "Brown footage," shot in 2008 during a Bigfoot Field Researchers Organization (BFRO) expedition, shows a large, man-like figure moving through the woods. While the footage isn't definitive, it represents the kind of potential evidence that thermal imaging can provide.

Another intriguing instance is the "thermal footage" from the TV show "Finding Bigfoot." Filmed in 2011 in North Carolina, it shows a large, bipedal creature briefly caught in the thermal camera. The size and behaviour of the figure led the team to assert that it could be a Sasquatch, sparking debate within the Bigfoot research community.

While thermal imaging has yet to provide clear, indisputable evidence of Bigfoot, its use represents a significant advance in research methodology. The shadows of heat captured by these cameras hold the promise of finally bringing Bigfoot out from the shadows of myth and into the light of scientific scrutiny.

# EDWARD TURNER

# Chapter 5: Hidden in Plain Sight: The Elusive Bigfoot

5.1 In Nature's Hideaway – The Habitats of Bigfoot

In the elusive hunt for Bigfoot, understanding the creature's purported habitat is crucial. As reports suggest, Bigfoot appears to favour dense forests, mountainous regions, and remote wilderness, drawing a compelling picture of a creature at home in the least disturbed corners of the North American landscape.

Foremost among these preferred habitats are dense forests. The Pacific Northwest, a region synonymous with Bigfoot, is carpeted with vast tracts of temperate rainforest, with ancient trees providing cover and an abundance of food resources. The Great Smoky Mountains, another hotspot, present a diverse deciduous forest, thick with undergrowth and blessed with plentiful water sources. In these dense forests, a large creature could conceivably move unseen, its presence betrayed only by occasional footprints or the eerie echo of a distant howl.

Mountainous regions also figure prominently in Bigfoot lore. The Himalayan Yeti, often considered a cousin to Bigfoot, is believed to reside in the harsh, isolated peaks of the world's highest mountain range. In North America, Bigfoot sightings are often clustered around mountain ranges, from the

Appalachians in the east to the Rockies in the west, and the Cascades and Sierras in between. These rugged landscapes, often draped in forests, offer isolation and a variety of potential food sources, making them a plausible habitat for an undiscovered primate.

Finally, the remote wilderness, untouched by human civilization, is often associated with Bigfoot sightings. The vast northern boreal forests, stretching across Canada and Alaska, are home to many reports. Similarly, the Florida Everglades, a unique wilderness of swamps and forests, has its own version of Bigfoot, known as the Skunk Ape. It seems that wherever there is wilderness, Bigfoot follows.

These wild, untouched habitats serve as a fitting backdrop for the mystery of Bigfoot, underlining the creature's association with the untouched and unknown. For those seeking this enigmatic creature, these landscapes offer more than just a hunting ground. They provide a connection to the wild, a stepping stone back to the time when unexplored territories covered the map, and unknown creatures roamed freely. In the dense forest shadows, across the craggy mountain scapes, and deep within the heart of the wilderness, the search for Bigfoot is as much an exploration of these last pockets of wild as it is a quest for the creature itself.

# 5.2 Hide and Seek - Bigfoot's Elusive Nature

AS MUCH AS WE'VE LEARNED about Bigfoot through decades of research and countless eyewitness accounts, the creature's elusive nature remains one of its defining characteristics. It's this tantalising dance of near-discovery that lends the Bigfoot enigma its enduring appeal. To understand why this creature remains so elusive, we must delve into the proposed behavioural traits that make Bigfoot difficult to detect and study: namely, its camouflage abilities, avoidance techniques, and nocturnal behaviour.

Bigfoot's ability to blend into its environment is often cited as a key factor in its elusiveness. This goes beyond the creature's reported physical attributes, such as its dark fur, which would allow it to blend seamlessly into the forest shadows. Some eyewitness accounts even suggest that Bigfoot may actively employ methods of camouflage, such as crouching among underbrush or hiding behind trees when humans are nearby. Additionally, there's speculation that Bigfoot may use natural features of the environment—like fallen trees or overgrown foliage—to conceal its tracks or nests, further thwarting efforts to locate it.

Another commonly proposed trait is Bigfoot's purportedly advanced avoidance techniques. Reports often describe the creature as being highly alert and sensitive to the presence of humans, displaying a remarkable ability to disappear quickly and silently. There are tales of Bigfoot disappearing in the blink of an eye, even in the face of multiple witnesses. This uncanny ability to evade detection, often described as almost supernatural, could be a combination of acute sensory abilities and an intimate knowledge of the terrain, both of which would be expected in a large, wild primate.

Adding to Bigfoot's elusive nature is the creature's purported nocturnal behaviour. Most Bigfoot sightings occur at dawn or dusk, suggesting that the creature is most active during these periods, much like many known primate species. Nocturnal behaviour would offer several advantages: it provides additional cover of darkness, it allows for quieter movement, and it coincides with the resting period of most humans, reducing chances of encounters.

These proposed behavioural traits, in combination with Bigfoot's preferred remote and rugged habitats, offer a compelling explanation as to why such a large creature has remained so tantalisingly out of reach. At the same time, these very characteristics stimulate our curiosity and our determination to uncover the truth about Bigfoot. After all, the thrill of the chase is often in the elusiveness of the quarry.

## 5.3 Footprints Across the Landscape - Bigfoot's Potential Migration Patterns and Geographic Range

AS WE TRAVERSE THE dense forests and rugged mountains in search of Bigfoot, a key question looms: does Bigfoot have a defined migration pattern or geographic range? By considering potential seasonal movements, territoriality, and adaptability to different environments, we may start to piece together a plausible picture of Bigfoot's movements across the American wilderness.

A common theory among researchers proposes seasonal movements for Bigfoot. This migratory pattern, seen in many animal species, is typically driven by food availability and weather conditions. Sightings of Bigfoot have fluctuated seasonally, with peaks in the warmer months. This could imply that Bigfoot migrates to higher elevations or more remote areas during summer, possibly in pursuit of certain food sources or to avoid human activity. Conversely, during winter, the creature might descend to lower elevations where conditions are less harsh, and food, albeit scarce, might be more accessible.

Territoriality is another aspect to consider. Many large mammals, such as bears and certain primates, exhibit territorial behaviour. If Bigfoot exhibits similar behaviour, it might have a specific home range that it patrols and defends. This could explain the recurrence of sightings in certain areas. Moreover, territorial markers attributed to Bigfoot, such as tree snaps or so-called "teepee" structures, have been interpreted by some researchers as signs of the creature marking its territory, much as other animals might leave scent marks or visual signs.

Finally, Bigfoot's adaptability to different environments might define its geographic range. Sightings have been reported from the rainforests of the Pacific Northwest to the swamps of Florida, suggesting that Bigfoot, if it exists, is remarkably adaptable. It would have to be comfortable both in dense forests and open mountain slopes, in both the humid heat of a southern summer and the biting cold of a northern winter. This adaptability would allow it to exploit a wide range of habitats, expanding its potential geographic range.

These theories, while speculative, offer intriguing insights into how Bigfoot might move across the landscape and where it might make its home. As we gather more evidence and refine our understanding, we may one day be able to sketch a map of Bigfoot's travels and territories. But for now, the creature's movements remain as mysterious and captivating as the creature itself.

## 5.4 The Bigfoot Ecosystem - Unseen Impact of an Unknown Species

IN OUR EXPLORATION of the Bigfoot enigma, we now venture into an intriguing avenue of inquiry - what ecological impact might this elusive creature have on its environment, and what potential role might it play in the ecosystem? To address these questions, we will ponder the creature's possible trophic level, its hypothetical prey selection, and its potential interactions with other species.

A creature's trophic level, or its position in the food chain, can offer insights into its ecological role. Given its purported size and physical capabilities, Bigfoot is often speculated to be an omnivore or even a top predator, similar to bears or great apes. As an omnivore, Bigfoot could play a vital role in controlling populations of certain prey species, perhaps small mammals or birds, as well as spreading seeds through its consumption of plant material. If it's a top predator, Bigfoot could have an even more profound effect on its environment by helping to regulate populations of larger animals, potentially including deer or elk.

Prey selection is closely related to a creature's trophic level and can further illuminate its ecological role. Reports and speculation surrounding Bigfoot suggest a diet that includes both plant and animal matter. Hypothetical signs of its feeding habits, such as stripped tree bark or devoured roadkill, hint at a creature capable of exploiting a range of food sources. Such an eclectic diet could allow Bigfoot to fill a niche similar to that of a bear or an ape, capitalising on a variety of resources according to seasonal availability.

Finally, Bigfoot's potential interactions with other species could reveal much about its ecological role. If Bigfoot behaves similarly to other large mammals, it may influence its environment in ways beyond its diet. For example, its movement through the underbrush might create "game trails" used by other species, or its digging for roots and tubers could aerate the soil, aiding in nutrient cycling. Additionally, by competing with other species for resources, it could indirectly shape the structure of local animal communities.

While the mystery of Bigfoot primarily stirs our curiosity and fuels our sense of wonder, contemplating its ecological role allows us to appreciate the creature in a broader context. As a potential inhabitant of North America's wild places, Bigfoot's existence would have far-reaching implications, not only reshaping our understanding of natural history but also reshaping the ecosystems it inhabits.

# Chapter 6: Cultural Impact and Popular Culture

## 6.1 Bigfoot in Literature and Folklore

As we journey deeper into the world of Bigfoot, it becomes increasingly clear that our fascination with this elusive creature extends far beyond the realm of cryptozoology and into the cultural sphere. From novels and short stories to poems and urban legends, Bigfoot has loomed large in the human imagination, becoming an emblem of the wild unknown and a vehicle for our deepest questions about nature and ourselves.

Bigfoot's literary footprint is as vast as the creature itself. In novels and short stories, Bigfoot often serves as a symbol of the wilderness and the mysteries it harbours. This can be seen in works like Elizabeth Marshall Thomas's "Reindeer Moon," where an ancient Bigfoot-like creature becomes a symbol of the primal forces that both challenge and sustain human life. In children's literature, such as R.L. Stine's "The Beast," Bigfoot is often depicted as a source of fear and excitement, mirroring our primal fear of what lurks in the forest, but also our child-like curiosity and sense of adventure.

Poetry, too, has been touched by the Bigfoot myth. Poets such as American Indian writer Sherman Alexie have drawn on Bigfoot to explore themes of identity and cultural heritage. In Alexie's "Reservation Sasquatch," Bigfoot is a symbol of the untamed spirit, a spectral presence that challenges the encroachment of modern life on traditional ways of living.

Perhaps most pervasive are the urban legends, the whispered tales that have spread across North America, passing from generation to generation. In these stories, Bigfoot can be a harbinger of doom, a guardian of the forest, or a lost soul wandering the wilderness. These legends resonate because they speak to universal human experiences: fear of the unknown, respect for nature, and empathy for the outsider.

Beyond literature, Bigfoot has permeated our culture in surprising ways. It has inspired numerous films, TV shows, and documentaries. It appears on merchandise ranging from t-shirts to coffee mugs. There are even Bigfoot-themed festivals, where enthusiasts gather to share their sightings, research, and love for this elusive creature.

Through all these portrayals, Bigfoot's cultural significance becomes clear. It is more than just a creature of myth and legend. It is a symbol of our relationship with the natural world, a mirror reflecting our fears and fascinations, our curiosity and our desire to understand the mysteries that still lie hidden in the heart of the wilderness.

Having examined Bigfoot's place in literature and its wider cultural significance, where shall we head next on our quest to unlock the mystery of Bigfoot?

## 6.2 Bigfoot on the Silver Screen -

# Representation in Movies and Documentaries

AS WE MOVE FORWARD in our exploration of Bigfoot's cultural resonance, we find ourselves in the realm of visual storytelling. Bigfoot's mysterious allure has inspired numerous portrayals on the silver screen, from heartwarming family comedies to chilling horror films, from groundbreaking documentaries to insightful TV specials. In this chapter, we will examine notable representations of Bigfoot in movies and documentaries, such as "Harry and the Hendersons," "Willow Creek," and famous documentaries that have tried to shed light on this elusive entity.

"Harry and the Hendersons" is a delightful 1987 family comedy that brought Bigfoot into the living rooms of mainstream America. The titular Harry, a friendly Bigfoot, accidentally becomes part of the Henderson family after they hit him with their car. Harry is portrayed as an intelligent, empathetic, and remarkably human character, reflecting our desire to find something familiar and relatable in the unknown. The movie fosters a sense of affection and respect for Bigfoot, a sharp contrast to the fear or menace the creature is often associated with in other portrayals.

On the opposite end of the spectrum lies "Willow Creek," a 2013 found-footage horror film directed by comedian Bobcat Goldthwait. In this chilling movie, Bigfoot is an unseen, malevolent force that terrorises a couple who venture into the creature's purported habitat to make a documentary. "Willow Creek" leverages the fear of the unknown and our primal unease about what might lurk unseen in the wilderness. Through suspenseful storytelling and clever use of sound design, the movie turns Bigfoot into an embodiment of our deepest fears.

Documentaries have also played a crucial role in shaping our perception of Bigfoot. Arguably the most famous is "Sasquatch: Legend Meets Science," a 2001 documentary that brings together experts in various fields to examine the evidence for Bigfoot's existence. Through a rigorous scientific lens, the film analyses footprint casts, hair samples, and the infamous Patterson-Gimlin film, fueling the debate with an objective, evidence-based approach.

Meanwhile, the proliferation of Bigfoot-themed TV specials and series, such as "Finding Bigfoot" and "Expedition Bigfoot," continue to stoke public interest in the creature. While these shows vary in their degree of scientific rigour, they provide a platform for eyewitness testimonies, share research findings, and often introduce a broader audience to the world of cryptozoology.

Bigfoot's varied representations in movies and documentaries reflect our complex relationship with this enigmatic creature. They highlight our curiosity, our fear, our longing for connection with the wild, and our persistent desire to probe the boundaries of the known world. As our exploration of the Bigfoot mystery continues, these portrayals serve as a testament to the enduring fascination Bigfoot holds in our cultural imagination.

# 6.3 Bigfoot Enthusiasts and Researchers -

# The Heartbeat of Cryptozoology

IN OUR EXPLORATION of the Bigfoot phenomenon, we come to recognize that this quest's true heartbeat lies within its dedicated community of enthusiasts and researchers. These individuals, driven by curiosity, passion, and a steadfast commitment to uncovering the truth, have played an invaluable role in maintaining the vigour of Bigfoot research and keeping the mystery alive. They've helped shape cryptozoology into a vibrant, albeit unorthodox, field of inquiry. In this chapter, we'll explore the various ways in which Bigfoot enthusiasts and researchers contribute to the community, including their participation in conferences and conventions, their hands-on field investigations, and their collaborative efforts.

Cryptozoology conferences and conventions, like the Ohio Bigfoot Conference or the International Cryptozoology Conference, serve as vital gathering points for the community. These events allow enthusiasts to engage with like-minded individuals, exchange ideas, present their findings, and learn from experts in the field. They often feature guest speakers, including prominent researchers, eyewitnesses, and even sceptics, providing a forum for diverse perspectives on the Bigfoot enigma.

However, the efforts of Bigfoot enthusiasts and researchers aren't confined to conference halls. Many conduct hands-on field investigations, venturing into the wilderness in search of the elusive creature. These investigations range from day-long trips to long-term expeditions, often involving rigorous hiking, overnight stakeouts, and detailed data collection. They scour the landscape for tracks, listen for vocalisations, set up trail cameras, and collect any potential evidence that could provide insights into Bigfoot's existence.

Moreover, the community is characterised by a spirit of collaboration. Enthusiasts and researchers often work together on field investigations, share their findings and theories online, and support each other's efforts in various ways. Online forums, social media groups, and websites like the Bigfoot Field Researchers Organization serve as platforms for this collaborative engagement. Through these collective efforts, the community fosters a sense of shared purpose and camaraderie, further fueling the quest for Bigfoot.

While the Bigfoot community's activities might not conform to conventional scientific norms, their contribution to our understanding of this elusive creature is undeniable. They keep the Bigfoot legend alive, inspire us to question our understanding of the natural world, and remind us that there are still mysteries out there, waiting to be discovered. In doing so, they embody the spirit of exploration and the relentless human desire to uncover the unknown.

## 6.4 The Public's Enduring Fascination - Bigfoot in the Media Spotlight

AS WE DELVE FURTHER into the phenomenon of Bigfoot, it becomes clear that the enduring public fascination with this elusive creature extends well beyond the sphere of cryptozoology. Whether it's breaking news of a possible sighting, a viral video purporting to show the creature in action, or a flurry

# BEYOND THE SHADOWS: UNLOCKING THE MYSTERY OF BIGFOOT

of social media discussions sparked by the latest research, Bigfoot has become a recurring feature in our media landscape. This chapter seeks to analyse the public's enduring fascination with Bigfoot and how this fascination is reflected and perpetuated by the media coverage it receives.

News reports play a significant role in shaping public perception of Bigfoot and maintaining interest in the creature. Whether it's a local newspaper reporting a recent sighting or a national news outlet covering a major development in Bigfoot research, these reports generate excitement, stoke curiosity, and often provoke debate. News coverage gives credence to eyewitness accounts and provides a platform for researchers to share their findings, further legitimising the quest for Bigfoot in the public's eye.

The advent of social media has only amplified the public's fascination with Bigfoot. Platforms like Facebook, Twitter, and Reddit are abuzz with discussions, debates, and shared experiences revolving around Bigfoot. These platforms allow enthusiasts to connect with each other, share their theories, disseminate their research, and provide a space for individuals to share their own encounters with the creature. It's through these online communities that many people find a supportive environment to indulge their interest in the Bigfoot mystery.

Perhaps the most potent contributor to Bigfoot's media presence are viral videos. From shaky, grainy footage of supposed Bigfoot encounters to meticulous breakdowns of the infamous Patterson-Gimlin film, these videos have become a staple of the digital age. Even though many of these videos are later debunked or viewed sceptically, they perpetuate the Bigfoot legend by sparking intrigue and capturing public attention.

In all of these, one thing is clear: the public's fascination with Bigfoot is not waning; if anything, it's growing. As new generations come of age in an era defined by digital communication and social sharing, Bigfoot's place in popular culture seems assured. The creature's enigma continues to engage our collective imagination, challenge our understanding of the natural world, and remind us that the world still holds mysteries that elude our grasp.

As we move forward in our journey to unlock the mystery of Bigfoot, the role of the media in shaping our perceptions and feeding our fascination with the creature is undeniable.

# Chapter 7: Cryptozoology and the Search for Hidden Species

## 7.1 Beyond Bigfoot - Other Fascinating Cryptids

As our exploration of Bigfoot reaches its peak, we step back to view the broader landscape of cryptids — creatures that, like Bigfoot, exist on the fringes of established science, yet persist in our collective consciousness. The world is filled with tales of cryptids that stir our curiosity, tantalise our imaginations, and challenge our understanding of the natural world. In this chapter, we will journey around the globe to meet some of these other fascinating cryptids: the Loch Ness Monster, the Chupacabra, the Mothman, and the Jersey Devil.

Nestled in the Scottish Highlands, the dark, deep waters of Loch Ness are said to harbour a mysterious creature known as the Loch Ness Monster, or "Nessie." Sightings date back to the 6th century, with a surge in modern interest following a purported photograph taken in 1934, famously known as "the Surgeon's Photo." Despite numerous expeditions employing the latest technology, Nessie continues to elude definitive detection, thus preserving the mystique that has made her a global icon.

Turning our gaze to the sunny climes of Puerto Rico and the southern United States, we encounter the Chupacabra, a creature of modern folklore. Descriptions of the Chupacabra vary, but it is often depicted as a heavy, spiky creature with piercing red eyes that preys on livestock. Reports of livestock found drained of blood, first in Puerto Rico in the mid-1990s and later in other places, have been attributed to this elusive beast.

Meanwhile, in West Virginia, locals whisper of a chilling apparition known as the Mothman. Described as a humanoid figure with glowing red eyes and massive wings, the Mothman first came into public consciousness following a series of sightings in the mid-1960s. The creature gained further notoriety when some linked its appearances to the tragic collapse of the Silver Bridge in 1967.

Lastly, we journey to the Pine Barrens of New Jersey, a setting steeped in folklore and home to the Jersey Devil. This creature, often depicted as a bipedal kangaroo-like entity with a horse or goat-like head, bat wings, horns, small arms with clawed hands, and a forked tail, has its roots in colonial-era tales. Sightings persist to this day, ensuring the Jersey Devil's place in America's rich tapestry of cryptid lore.

These cryptids, along with Bigfoot, illustrate our inherent fascination with the unknown and the unexplained. They remind us that the world is full of mysteries waiting to be explored, that our understanding of the natural world is continually evolving, and that there is always room for wonder and speculation. Our journey beyond the shadows of Bigfoot has revealed a world teeming with cryptids just as captivating and enigmatic.

# 7.2 Cryptozoology Unveiled - Organizations and Individuals Pioneering the Unknown

BEYOND THE INTRIGUING realm of Bigfoot and its cryptid kin, we find a broader field dedicated to studying such elusive creatures. This field, known as cryptozoology, holds a world of mystery, curiosity, and relentless pursuit of knowledge. From independent researchers to professional organisations, countless individuals and groups dedicate their time, resources, and expertise to uncovering the truth about these unknown creatures. In this chapter, we'll venture into the world of cryptozoology, exploring key organisations like the International Cryptozoology Museum and the Centre for Fortean Zoology, as well as influential individuals like Loren Coleman.

The International Cryptozoology Museum, located in Portland, Maine, serves as a beacon for enthusiasts and researchers worldwide. Founded by renowned cryptozoologist Loren Coleman in 2003, the museum houses an extensive collection of cryptid artefacts, specimens, and pop culture items. Its exhibits span the spectrum of cryptozoology, from well-known creatures like Bigfoot and Nessie to lesser-known entities from around the globe. Through its efforts, the museum seeks to educate the public about cryptozoology and its contributions, fostering a sense of wonder and curiosity about the world's unexplained creatures.

On the other side of the Atlantic, the Centre for Fortean Zoology (CFZ) in the United Kingdom conducts research and investigations into unknown animals. Named after Charles Fort, a writer known for his collections of anomalous phenomena, the CFZ has been at the forefront of cryptozoological research since its inception in 1992. It organises expeditions around the world, publishes books and a journal, and hosts the annual Weird Weekend conference, all with the goal of advancing our understanding of cryptids.

Among the pioneers in the field of cryptozoology, Loren Coleman stands out. A prominent cryptozoologist, author, and founder of the International Cryptozoology Museum, Coleman has devoted his life to the study of unknown creatures. His extensive research and publications have greatly contributed to the field, earning him recognition as one of the world's leading cryptozoologists. His relentless dedication embodies the spirit of cryptozoology, inspiring a new generation of researchers.

The realm of cryptozoology is vast, extending far beyond the shadowy figure of Bigfoot. It represents an ongoing quest for knowledge, an attempt to shed light on the mysteries that elude conventional science. Through the efforts of organisations like the International Cryptozoology Museum and the Centre for Fortean Zoology, along with individuals like Loren Coleman, cryptozoology continues to thrive, challenging us to rethink what we know about the natural world.

# 7.3 Unsettling Uncertainties - High Profile Cases in Cryptozoology

CRYPTOZOOLOGY IS A field that is often defined by the cases it investigates. While creatures like Bigfoot, Nessie, and the Chupacabra are the headliners, there are countless other cryptids that have captured public interest and sparked considerable debate. These cases, ranging from menacing predators to enigmatic enigmas, showcase the diversity and fascination within the field. In this chapter, we'll discuss three such cases: The Beast of Bray Road, the Mongolian Death Worm, and the Marozi.

Situated in rural Wisconsin, Bray Road is an unassuming stretch of highway that has gained a sinister reputation due to the creature known as the Beast of Bray Road. Described as a large, muscular, wolf-like creature that walks on its hind legs, this Beast first captured public attention in the 1990s when a series of sightings were reported to the local newspaper. This led to an investigation by journalist Linda Godfrey, who popularised the creature and further cemented its place in the annals of cryptozoology. Despite years of investigations, the Beast remains an enigma, perpetuating fear and fascination in equal measure.

Far from the rural landscapes of Wisconsin, the arid expanses of the Gobi Desert play host to another cryptid, one known for its lethality: the Mongolian Death Worm. According to local legends, this creature, measuring up to two metres long and resembling a large, smooth worm, is capable of spewing acid and emitting lethal electric shocks. Though many Western expeditions have sought the creature, the Death Worm continues to evade definitive discovery, rendering it a captivating mystery in the world of cryptozoology.

From the deserts of Mongolia, we shift to the dense forests of East Africa, where we find the Marozi or the Spotted Lion. Unlike the terrifying visages of the Beast of Bray Road and the

Mongolian Death Worm, the Marozi is described as a small, spotted lion, a sort of hybrid between a leopard and a lion. Sightings of the Marozi date back to the early 20th century, with some evidence in the form of skins and skulls suggesting its existence. However, conclusive proof and live sightings have been elusive, adding to the enigma of the Marozi.

These cases represent just a fraction of the diverse cryptids that populate the field of cryptozoology. Each offers a tantalising glimpse into the unknown, challenging our understanding of the natural world and igniting our curiosity. They demonstrate that the world is full of unsolved mysteries, waiting to be uncovered and understood.

# 7.4 Bridging Realms - Fostering Collaboration between Cryptozoology and Mainstream Science

CRYPTOZOOLOGY, WHILE fascinating and compelling, has often found itself at odds with mainstream science. Critics point to a lack of empirical evidence, while supporters argue that scientific dogma can blind researchers to the possibility of unknown creatures. Yet, in recent years, there has been an increasing effort to bridge this divide, bringing cryptozoology closer to the methodologies and recognition of mainstream scientific disciplines. This chapter explores these ongoing efforts, focusing on citizen science initiatives, interdisciplinary collaborations, and the importance of peer-reviewed publications.

# BEYOND THE SHADOWS: UNLOCKING THE MYSTERY OF BIGFOOT

Citizen science initiatives have proven to be a significant boon to cryptozoology. These efforts involve everyday people in scientific research, expanding the range of data collection and fostering a deeper appreciation for science among the public. In the realm of cryptozoology, such initiatives have facilitated the collection of a wide array of potential evidence, from footprint casts to hair samples to sighting reports. Moreover, they have cultivated a network of individuals passionate about unravelling the mysteries of cryptids, bolstering the field's visibility and credibility.

Interdisciplinary collaboration is another important stride in bridging the gap between cryptozoology and mainstream science. By integrating perspectives from biology, anthropology, psychology, and other disciplines, cryptozoology can contribute unique insights to these fields while also benefiting from their methodologies and expertise. Such collaboration has already borne fruit in areas like primate research and folklore studies, where insights gleaned from cryptozoological investigations have provided new avenues for exploration.

Peer-reviewed publications serve as the gold standard for scientific research, and cryptozoology is no exception. Although traditionally underrepresented in these platforms, there has been an uptick in cryptozoological studies appearing in respected journals. These articles, which undergo rigorous review by experts in relevant fields, help validate cryptozoology as a serious scientific pursuit. They also provide a conduit for dialogue and critique, fostering growth and refinement within the field.

These initiatives are not without challenges, and the road to reconciliation between cryptozoology and mainstream science is still being paved. Yet, the strides made thus far are promising. They reflect an evolving understanding and acceptance of cryptozoology as a legitimate, valuable contribution to our collective scientific knowledge. As we continue to venture beyond the shadows, it's clear that the future of cryptozoology is not only about unearthing unknown creatures but also about finding its rightful place within the broader scientific community.

# Chapter 8: Bigfoot Hoaxes and Misidentifications

## 8.1 Deception and Trickery - Notable Bigfoot Hoaxes

In the swirling maelstrom of fascination, curiosity, and fear that surrounds Bigfoot, there are those who seek to exploit these feelings for personal gain or amusement. While the majority of Bigfoot enthusiasts and researchers are sincere in their interests, the field has not been immune to deliberate hoaxes. In this chapter, we will expose two of the most notable instances of such deception: the hoax perpetrated by Ray Wallace and the infamous Georgia Bigfoot hoax.

Ray Wallace was a construction worker from Washington state whose influence on the Bigfoot legend is undeniable. In the late 1950s, gigantic footprints appeared around construction sites where Wallace was working, stirring considerable intrigue and excitement. This marked the birth of 'Bigfoot', the term being coined by a local journalist covering the phenomenon. However, after Wallace's death in 2002, his family revealed that the footprints were a hoax. Using carved wooden feet, Wallace had been responsible for creating the massive prints. While his mischief has had a profound impact on Bigfoot lore, it also serves as a reminder of the susceptibility of the field to deception.

In 2008, the world of cryptozoology was rocked by what seemed to be a remarkable discovery. Two men from Georgia, Matthew Whitton and Rick Dyer, claimed to have found the body of a Bigfoot. They released photographs of the creature encased in ice and held a press conference announcing their find, creating a media frenzy. However, when the body was thawed for examination, it was revealed to be a rubber costume stuffed with animal parts. The Georgia Bigfoot hoax, as it came to be known, was a stark reminder of the need for rigorous verification in the field of cryptozoology.

These hoaxes serve as sobering examples of the challenges faced by serious researchers and enthusiasts within the Bigfoot community. They highlight the need for scepticism and rigorous scientific inquiry in the face of extraordinary claims. Yet, they also underscore the enduring fascination with Bigfoot, a fascination potent enough to drive individuals to such elaborate deceptions.

## 8.2 Echoes of the Familiar - Animals and Phenomena Mistaken for Bigfoot

IN THE WORLD OF CRYPTOZOOLOGY, and especially in the quest to prove the existence of Bigfoot, one key factor can often lead to misinterpretations and misidentifications: our mind's eagerness to see what it wants to see. Common animals and natural phenomena, viewed under the right circumstances, can easily be mistaken for the legendary creature. In this chapter, we delve into some of these sources of confusion, including bears, large canids, misshapen trees, and the psychological phenomenon known as pareidolia.

Bears, in particular, are frequently mistaken for Bigfoot. Standing on their hind legs, bears can reach impressive heights, and their footprint, while distinct to the trained eye, can resemble a hominid's under certain conditions. Their furred bodies, shuffling gait, and tendency to inhabit the same remote wilderness areas as Bigfoot is purported to, all contribute to their misidentification.

Similarly, large canids like wolves and coyotes can also be mistaken for Bigfoot, particularly when viewed from a distance or in poor lighting conditions. Their eyeshine, captured by flashlights or cameras, can be misinterpreted as the glowing eyes often attributed to Bigfoot.

An oddly shaped tree or stump can also trigger false sightings. In the dense, shadowy expanses of the forest, it's easy to misinterpret a silhouette or an unexpected movement. A gnarled tree trunk, an irregularly shaped stump, or even a cluster of foliage can, under the right circumstances, transform into a Bigfoot in the eyes of an eager observer.

All of these misidentifications tie into a broader psychological phenomenon called pareidolia. This is the tendency of the human mind to perceive patterns where none exist, such as seeing faces in clouds or hearing voices in static. It's thought that pareidolia may play a significant role in Bigfoot sightings, transforming innocuous sights and sounds into encounters with the legendary creature.

In our journey towards understanding Bigfoot, it is essential to separate the wheat from the chaff, the real from the imaginary, and the ordinary from the extraordinary. In the pursuit of truth, we must keep our feet grounded even as our imaginations reach towards the unknown.

## 8.3 Controversies and Scepticism - The Challenges of Bigfoot Research

OUR EXPLORATION OF Bigfoot and the realm of cryptozoology would be incomplete without addressing the controversies and scepticism that shadow these fields. From accusations of confirmation bias to the absence of scientific consensus and numerous debunking attempts, these issues are integral to our understanding of the Bigfoot enigma. In this chapter, we'll delve into these controversies, striving to provide a balanced view of the challenges that permeate Bigfoot research.

One common critique of Bigfoot enthusiasts and researchers is the claim of confirmation bias. This cognitive bias involves favouring information that confirms preexisting beliefs while ignoring or dismissing contradictory evidence. Some critics argue that this bias is prevalent in Bigfoot research, with enthusiasts more likely to interpret ambiguous evidence as supporting the creature's existence. However, it's worth noting that confirmation bias isn't unique to Bigfoot enthusiasts - it's a widespread human tendency that impacts all fields of study, from science to politics.

The lack of scientific consensus on Bigfoot's existence is another contentious issue. Mainstream scientists typically argue that without tangible, irrefutable evidence—such as a specimen for study—claims of Bigfoot's existence remain purely speculative. This demand for definitive proof is consistent with the scientific method, which values empirical evidence and reproducibility. However, Bigfoot researchers point out that many animals were once considered myths before their eventual discovery, arguing that the lack of a specimen doesn't necessarily negate Bigfoot's existence.

Debunking attempts also contribute to the controversy surrounding Bigfoot. Many have sought to disprove specific sightings or pieces of evidence, often attributing them to hoaxes, misidentification, or natural phenomena. These debunking attempts serve a crucial role in sifting fact from fiction and ensuring the integrity of Bigfoot research. However, they can also inadvertently dismiss genuine evidence, particularly when applied too broadly or without sufficient consideration of the specifics of each case.

These controversies and the scepticism they engender form an essential part of the Bigfoot narrative. They illustrate the ongoing tension between belief and scepticism, between the known and the unknown. Above all, they underscore the importance of maintaining an open yet critical mind, of balancing curiosity with discernment, in our pursuit of the truth about Bigfoot.

# 8.4 The Dance of Discernment - Critical Thinking in Bigfoot Research

IN THE QUEST TO UNCOVER the truth about Bigfoot, two elements prove to be indispensable guides: critical thinking and scepticism. These two tools help ensure that the pursuit of Bigfoot doesn't stray into the realm of unfounded belief or blind acceptance but remains grounded in rigorous investigation and objective analysis. In this chapter, we explore the vital roles of critical thinking and scepticism in analysing Bigfoot evidence, avoiding confirmation bias, and embracing the peer review process.

The first step in applying critical thinking to Bigfoot research is to approach every piece of evidence with an open but questioning mind. This approach involves examining the evidence from multiple perspectives, asking probing questions, and looking for potential flaws or inconsistencies. It's not about debunking for the sake of debunking but rather about seeking truth, no matter where that quest may lead.

This kind of rigorous analysis is vital in avoiding confirmation bias, which we discussed in the previous chapter. By consciously striving to view evidence objectively, researchers can guard against the human tendency to see what we want to see. Every claim of a Bigfoot sighting or piece of evidence should be weighed against alternative explanations. Could that large, shadowy figure in the forest be a bear? Could the mysterious sounds be attributable to known animals or natural phenomena? Could the gigantic footprints be a prank or a misinterpretation of natural markings?

# BEYOND THE SHADOWS: UNLOCKING THE MYSTERY OF BIGFOOT

One of the most powerful tools in the quest for truth is the process of peer review. By sharing their findings with others in the field, researchers expose their work to critique and questioning. This can be a humbling process, as cherished theories may be challenged and unexpected flaws revealed. Yet, this is also a strengthening process. Through the crucible of peer review, ideas are refined, assumptions are challenged, and the understanding of Bigfoot – and the mystery that surrounds it – deepens.

Critical thinking and scepticism are not enemies of Bigfoot research; rather, they are its allies. They help to clear the path of unfounded claims and dubious evidence, leaving the way open for genuine discoveries. They enable researchers to approach the mystery of Bigfoot with a balance of open-minded curiosity and discerning scrutiny.

# Chapter 9: Beyond Bigfoot: Exploring Other Enigmatic Creatures

## 9.1 The Abominable Snowman – Legends and Evidence of the Yeti

As we broaden our understanding of the Bigfoot phenomenon, we must turn our gaze to distant lands, where tales of other enigmatic creatures echo through ancient mountains and vast forests. One of these creatures is the Yeti, or the 'Abominable Snowman', as it's often called in the West. This legendary creature is said to roam the icy peaks and valleys of the Himalayas, and like Bigfoot, it stands at the intersection of folklore, eyewitness accounts, and disputed physical evidence. In this chapter, we delve into the enigma of the Yeti, exploring Sherpa testimonies, footprint discoveries, and the many expeditions to Mount Everest in search of this elusive creature.

The Yeti is deeply woven into the fabric of Sherpa culture. These indigenous people of the Himalayas have spoken of the Yeti for centuries, depicting it as a powerful and elusive creature that treads the boundary between the human and animal worlds. The Sherpa testimonies vary, with some describing the Yeti as a benevolent protector of the mountains, while others speak of a more menacing creature.

One of the most tangible and controversial aspects of the Yeti phenomenon is the discovery of alleged footprints in the snow.

These footprints, often larger and broader than a human's, have been photographed and cast by various expeditions. Yet, their origin remains a subject of heated debate. While some argue they belong to the elusive Yeti, others suggest they could be the tracks of known animals, distorted and enlarged by the melting snow.

Mount Everest, the tallest peak in the world, has long been a focal point for Yeti expeditions. From the early 20th century to the present day, mountaineers and researchers have ventured into the harsh, high-altitude wilderness in search of the creature. Notable among these was the 1951 Mount Everest expedition led by Eric Shipton, which brought back photographs of mysterious footprints that sparked a global Yeti craze.

Despite countless expeditions and the accumulation of testimonies and alleged evidence, the existence of the Yeti remains a question shrouded in mystery. The Himalayas, with their extreme weather, treacherous terrain, and sparse population, offer a perfect refuge for a creature seeking to evade human detection. Whether the Yeti is a yet-undiscovered species, a misidentified known animal, a product of high-altitude hallucinations, or a symbol of the wild, untamed spirit of the Himalayas, remains to be seen.

As we venture deeper into the realms of mystery and legend, we invite you to join us in exploring the connections, contrasts, and conundrums between Bigfoot, the Yeti, and other cryptids that roam our collective imagination.

# 9.2 From the Depths - The Loch Ness Monster

FROM THE TOWERING HEIGHTS of the Himalayas, we journey to the depths of a vast, murky loch in the Scottish Highlands. Here, amidst rolling hills and under frequently grey skies, lurks a creature whose reputation rivals that of Bigfoot and the Yeti - the Loch Ness Monster, affectionately known as Nessie. This chapter plunges into the mythology and scientific investigations surrounding this elusive aquatic creature, delving into sightings, photographs, sonar scans, and the work of the Loch Ness Investigation Bureau.

The first recorded sighting of Nessie dates back to the 6th century in a text documenting the life of Saint Columba. Yet, it was in the 1930s that Nessie truly swam into the public consciousness, following a series of sightings and the publication of the now-infamous "Surgeon's Photograph". This image, though later revealed as a hoax, served to cement Nessie's place in modern folklore and sparked a surge of interest in the creature.

Sightings of Nessie, often described as a large creature with a long neck and one or more humps protruding from the water, have continued to the present day. They provide tantalising, though often frustratingly vague, pieces of the puzzle. Could Nessie be a relic population of plesiosaurs, marine reptiles thought to have gone extinct along with the dinosaurs? Or perhaps a giant eel, or even an optical illusion caused by boat wakes or floating debris?

Intriguing as these sightings are, the Loch Ness Monster hasn't only been sought with the naked eye. Sonar scans of the loch have played a significant role in the hunt for Nessie. Over the decades, several expeditions have detected large, unexplained objects moving beneath the loch's surface. While these findings have sparked excitement, they remain open to interpretation, and concrete evidence eludes us.

Founded in the 1960s, the Loch Ness Investigation Bureau aimed to apply a systematic, scientific approach to the hunt for Nessie. Volunteers kept a continuous watch over the loch and took photographs, hoping to catch a glimpse of the elusive creature. While the Bureau was disbanded in the 1970s, its mission to understand the mysteries of Loch Ness continues to inspire researchers today.

The Loch Ness Monster stands as a captivating symbol of the unknown lurking beneath the surface, a reminder of the mysteries that our world still holds. Whether a real creature, a misidentified phenomenon, or a beloved legend, Nessie continues to capture our imaginations and fuel our desire for discovery.

# 9.3 The Goat Sucker - Origins and Encounters with the Chupacabra

AS WE TRAVEL FURTHER into the realm of cryptids, we cross the Atlantic and journey to Latin America, a land rich in folklore and legend. Here, amidst the vibrant cultures and diverse landscapes, we encounter a creature both chilling and fascinating - the Chupacabra, or 'goat sucker'. In this chapter, we uncover the origins of this elusive creature, delve into tales of strange mutilated livestock, and explore how vampire legends and cryptid investigations intertwine in the enigma of the Chupacabra.

The Chupacabra first emerged in Puerto Rico in the mid-1990s, when farmers began finding their livestock – particularly goats – drained of blood and bearing strange puncture wounds. These eerie discoveries sparked widespread fear and speculation about a new and terrifying predator. The creature was soon dubbed the Chupacabra, a name derived from its alleged habit of sucking the blood from goats.

Descriptions of the Chupacabra vary, with some eyewitnesses describing a creature about the size of a small bear, with a row of spines down its back, while others report seeing a strange breed of wild dog. Despite these variations, the accounts share one common and chilling detail: the Chupacabra's predilection for livestock and its vampiric method of killing.

The tale of the Chupacabra has similarities to age-old vampire legends. Vampires, creatures of the night known for sucking the blood of the living, have been a part of folklore across the world for centuries. The Chupacabra, with its nocturnal habits and blood-sucking tendencies, seems to embody this archetype in a uniquely Latin American context.

Since the first reports in Puerto Rico, sightings of the Chupacabra have spread throughout Latin America and into the Southern United States. Numerous investigations have been launched to unravel the truth behind this cryptid. However, concrete evidence remains elusive. Some suggest that the mutilated livestock could be the work of known predators or a result of natural diseases. Others, however, remain convinced that a yet-unexplained creature is to blame.

The Chupacabra serves as a stark reminder that the world is still filled with unsolved mysteries and unexplored frontiers. Its tale is a testament to the power of folklore in shaping our perceptions of the unknown and our never-ending quest to understand the mysteries of the natural world.

# 9.4 Wings and Hooves - The Mothman and Jersey Devil

FROM THE DEPTHS OF Loch Ness to the blood-sucking Chupacabra of Latin America, our exploration of cryptids continues. As we return to the United States, we find ourselves delving into two other beguiling legends: the Mothman of West Virginia and the Jersey Devil in New Jersey. In this chapter, we explore these two intriguing cryptids, unearthing regional myths, legends, and sightings that continue to captivate the public.

The Mothman, an enigmatic creature reported to have terrorised the small town of Point Pleasant, West Virginia, in the late 1960s, is a truly fascinating cryptid. Described as a humanoid figure with wings spanning up to ten feet and possessing glowing red eyes, the Mothman is said to be a harbinger of doom. Sightings of this creature were linked to the tragic collapse of the Silver Bridge, which killed 46 people, leading to speculation that the Mothman's presence was an ominous precursor to the disaster. Despite numerous investigations and intense media interest, the true nature and origin of the Mothman remain shrouded in mystery.

Across the Appalachians and into the Pine Barrens of New Jersey, the tale of another strange creature emerges: the Jersey Devil. Unlike the Mothman, the Jersey Devil is said to have haunted these parts for centuries. According to popular folklore, the Jersey Devil was the 13th child of Mother Leeds in 1735, cursed and transformed into a creature with hooves, a goat's head, bat wings, and a forked tail. Over the years, sightings of this strange beast have continued, leading to a mix of fear, scepticism, and intrigue.

Both the Mothman and Jersey Devil provide fascinating insights into regional myths and legends. They represent a complex blend of historical events, local culture, fear of the unknown, and the ever-present human tendency to ascribe the inexplicable to supernatural or unknown creatures. Cryptozoologists, historians, and folklorists alike continue to investigate these tales, searching for threads of truth amidst the fabric of myth and legend.

These stories serve as a testament to the enduring human fascination with the unexplained. As we continue to investigate Bigfoot and other cryptids worldwide, we are reminded that our quest for understanding the unknown is a journey without end.

# Chapter 10: Bigfoot in the Future: Unveiling the Truth

## 10.1 Looking Ahead - Future Technologies in Bigfoot Research

As we turn towards the future, our quest to uncover the mystery of Bigfoot is far from over. Modern technology and scientific advancements have already greatly assisted in our understanding of this elusive creature, and as we look forward, more innovative methods are on the horizon. This chapter delves into the cutting-edge technologies and techniques that hold promise for future Bigfoot research, including DNA barcoding, aerial surveys, and advanced camera traps.

DNA barcoding, a technique used to identify species based on a short DNA sequence, is an exciting advancement with potential applications for Bigfoot research. As it becomes increasingly affordable and accessible, researchers could analyse samples collected in the field, such as hair or skin, to match them against a vast database of known species. In the case of Bigfoot, an unknown or unusual DNA sequence could provide compelling evidence of its existence.

Next, we consider aerial surveys, particularly those conducted with unmanned aerial vehicles (UAVs), also known as drones. Drones can cover large areas of rugged or inaccessible terrain, capturing high-resolution imagery that can be scrutinised for signs of Bigfoot. Equipped with infrared or thermal imaging, drones could potentially detect the heat signature of a large creature, even under the forest canopy or in the darkness of night.

Finally, advancements in camera trap technology offer great potential. Camera traps, often used in wildlife research, are motion-activated cameras that can be left in the field for extended periods. Newer models are equipped with night vision, operate silently, and can transmit images in real time. Deploying advanced camera traps in areas of reported Bigfoot activity could yield clear, indisputable photographic evidence.

Alongside these technologies, the future of Bigfoot research will also depend on continued collaboration between scientists, amateur researchers, and local communities. Citizen science initiatives, where members of the public contribute to data collection and analysis, will also be instrumental in gathering large amounts of information from across vast geographical areas.

With these technologies and techniques, we stand at the threshold of a new era in Bigfoot research, one that promises deeper insights and, possibly, concrete evidence. The road ahead is full of potential, and our journey to unlock the mystery of Bigfoot and other cryptids continues.

# 10.2 United in Pursuit - The Power of Collaboration and Knowledge Sharing

THE WORLD OF CRYPTID research, with its unique challenges and distinctive subject matter, isn't a realm for lone wolves. The complexity and global scope of phenomena like Bigfoot demand a collaborative, interconnected approach, one that draws upon the strengths of researchers from diverse backgrounds and areas of expertise. In this chapter, we will explore the importance of collaboration and knowledge sharing among researchers, focusing on the value of international research networks, shared databases, and open-access publications.

International research networks are essential in the pursuit of elusive cryptids like Bigfoot. They provide a platform for researchers from around the world to connect, share findings, and collaborate on projects. By transcending geographic and cultural boundaries, these networks allow for a diverse, multi-faceted approach to understanding Bigfoot, drawing on a wealth of cultural, historical, and scientific knowledge. Moreover, international collaboration can help address biases or blind spots that may exist within any single cultural or disciplinary perspective, ensuring a more balanced and comprehensive understanding of the phenomenon.

Shared databases are another vital tool for collaboration. These repositories enable researchers to access and analyse data collected by others, promoting transparency and reducing duplication of effort. For instance, a global database of Bigfoot sightings could offer valuable insights into patterns and trends, potentially revealing clues about the creature's behaviour, habitat, or migratory patterns. Furthermore, DNA databases, like those used in DNA barcoding, could provide a centralised resource for genetic data related to potential Bigfoot samples.

Open-access publications play a significant role in fostering knowledge sharing. By making research findings freely available to all, these publications ensure that knowledge is spread widely and is not confined within the walls of academia. This is particularly important in a field like Bigfoot research, where amateur enthusiasts often make significant contributions. Accessible, peer-reviewed research can help raise the standards of evidence and analysis throughout the community.

Collaboration and knowledge sharing are key to progressing in the complex and fascinating field of Bigfoot research. By working together, sharing findings openly, and building on each other's work, researchers can enhance our collective understanding of this enduring mystery. As we continue this journey into the unknown, the importance of unity in our pursuit of knowledge becomes increasingly evident.

## 10.3 Public Engagement - The Role of Citizen Science in Bigfoot Research

AS OUR JOURNEY INTO the mysteries of Bigfoot continues, we must acknowledge a crucial driving force behind this endeavour – the interest and participation of the general public. In this chapter, we delve into the role of public interest and citizen science in advancing Bigfoot research, emphasising the value of crowd-sourced data collection, community engagement, and public funding initiatives.

In the era of the Internet and smartphones, anyone can potentially contribute to the field of Bigfoot research. Crowd-sourced data collection, a staple of many citizen science initiatives, invites individuals from all walks of life to submit their own observations or findings. This could range from reporting a suspected sighting to sharing photos of unusual tracks or potential nesting sites. By harnessing the power of crowd-sourced data, researchers can tap into a vast network of observers spread across different regions and environments, greatly expanding the scope and reach of their investigations.

Community engagement goes beyond data collection. It also involves building relationships with local communities, fostering an environment of trust and mutual respect. Residents in areas of frequent Bigfoot sightings often have deep ties to the land and a wealth of local knowledge that can provide invaluable insights for researchers. By engaging with these communities, researchers can gain access to a rich tapestry of stories, observations, and experiences that might otherwise remain unheard.

Public funding initiatives also play a crucial role. Research, especially when it involves fieldwork and advanced technologies, can be costly. Public interest in Bigfoot has often translated into financial support, whether through crowdfunding platforms, donations, or grants from organisations interested in cryptozoology. This funding enables researchers to undertake more ambitious projects, employ more sophisticated technologies, and delve deeper into the mystery of Bigfoot.

Public interest and citizen science hold great potential for advancing Bigfoot research. By harnessing the collective power of interested individuals and communities, we can continue to push the boundaries of what we know and understand about this elusive creature. As we journey further into the shadowy realms of Bigfoot's existence, we are reminded that this endeavour is not a solitary quest but a collective exploration driven by curiosity, passion, and the pursuit of knowledge.

## 10.4 The Ripple Effect - The Potential Consequences of Proving or Disproving Bigfoot's Existence

THE HUNT FOR BIGFOOT has captivated imaginations for decades, but what would happen if we definitively proved or disproved its existence? The confirmation or denial of this elusive creature would not just make headlines around the world; it would send shockwaves through various sectors of society and science, causing significant ecological, cultural, and academic shifts. This chapter speculates on these potential consequences.

First, let's imagine that Bigfoot's existence is irrefutably confirmed. From an ecological perspective, the discovery of a previously unidentified large primate species in North America would revolutionise our understanding of the continent's biodiversity. Conservation efforts would likely need to be initiated to protect this species and its habitat, as Bigfoot's existence would raise questions about its population size, distribution, and ecological role. The discovery would also challenge established theories about primate evolution and biogeography, opening up new areas of study and research.

Culturally, the impact would be profound. Bigfoot, a figure entrenched in folklore, would transition from myth to reality, altering narratives in literature, film, and popular culture. The creature's cultural significance, particularly within indigenous communities, might also be reevaluated in light of its confirmed existence.

In the realm of cryptozoology, validating the existence of Bigfoot could lead to increased funding, credibility, and public interest in the field. Other cryptids might gain more serious attention, leading to an upsurge in research and exploration. Proving Bigfoot's existence could potentially bridge the gap between cryptozoology and mainstream science, paving the way for more collaborative and interdisciplinary research.

On the other hand, if Bigfoot were definitively disproved, the implications would be equally significant, albeit different. Ecologically, the debunking could lead to shifts in focus towards the conservation of known species and ecosystems, rather than speculative ones.

Culturally, Bigfoot would remain a powerful symbol and legend, but its status would likely evolve, potentially becoming a cautionary tale about the lines between fact and fiction, science and folklore. The story of Bigfoot might serve as a reminder of our penchant for myth-making and our enduring fascination with the unknown.

For cryptozoology, a definitive disproof of Bigfoot might lead to greater scrutiny and scepticism. However, it could also inspire more rigorous research methodologies and promote critical thinking within the field. Despite potential setbacks, the quest for understanding unknown creatures would likely continue, fueled by the enduring human curiosity for the mysterious and unexplained.

In the end, whether Bigfoot is proven or disproven, the impact of the conclusion will ripple out, influencing science, culture, and our understanding of the natural world. As we turn the page, we continue our exploration, eagerly anticipating the revelations yet to come.

# Conclusion: The Journey Thus Far - Reflections and the Enduring Allure of Bigfoot

As our exploration into the enigmatic world of Bigfoot draws to a close, it's time to pause, reflect, and consolidate our journey's key findings. We've navigated through the fascinating twists and turns of cultural histories, personal testimonies, research advances, and even the provocative world of hoaxes. Our expedition into this mystery, however, leaves us with many remaining questions, reminding us that the allure of Bigfoot endures as powerfully as ever.

Our journey has underscored the deep roots of Bigfoot in various cultures, particularly among indigenous communities in North America. We've also noted intriguing parallels in the folklore of other regions worldwide, hinting at a shared human fascination with elusive, large humanoid creatures. We've dissected numerous accounts, tracing back centuries, and discovered a wealth of personal testimonies that reflect a remarkably consistent narrative of encounters with this creature. This enduring narrative, bridging time and space, points to something that transcends mere coincidence or fancy.

We've celebrated the pioneering efforts of researchers like Ivan T. Sanderson, John Green, and René Dahinden, who laid the foundation for serious Bigfoot research. We've also ventured into the wilderness alongside various expeditions and noted their key findings, particularly the intriguing Patterson-Gimlin film and Freeman footage. The tireless dedication of these enthusiasts, both professional and amateur, has undoubtedly enriched our understanding and expanded our knowledge of this elusive creature.

In the face of technological advancements, we've seen how the field has evolved and adapted, using everything from night vision equipment to drones, from trail cameras to advanced audio recording devices. The contribution of technology to the search for Bigfoot cannot be overstated; it has revolutionised the way we investigate and record potential evidence.

However, despite all our findings, numerous questions remain. The fundamental one being - Does Bigfoot indeed exist? The evidence, as intriguing and compelling as it may be, is still not definitive. The search for irrefutable proof continues, and so does our exploration. How does Bigfoot fit into our ecosystem, if it exists at all? How does it interact with other species? What could its existence imply about primate evolution and biogeography?

The implications of our journey extend beyond the world of cryptozoology, touching upon broader themes in science, society, and culture. The enduring allure of Bigfoot goes beyond the thrill of the hunt or the fascination with the unknown. It speaks to our collective curiosity, our desire to understand our place in the world, and our insatiable hunger for exploration and discovery.

The mystery of Bigfoot, far from being a mere curiosity, is a potent symbol of our eternal quest for knowledge and understanding. It encapsulates our thirst for exploring the unknown and challenging the boundaries of established knowledge. And as long as there are mysteries to unravel and horizons to explore, the allure of Bigfoot will continue to captivate us, guiding us further into the uncharted territories of our understanding and curiosity.

As our exploration ends, we stand not at the conclusion but at a vista filled with infinite possibilities. The quest for Bigfoot is far from over, and the story continues, just beyond the shadows.

# Don't miss out!

Visit the website below and you can sign up to receive emails whenever Edward Turner publishes a new book. There's no charge and no obligation.

https://books2read.com/r/B-A-SYIZ-LUKLC

Connecting independent readers to independent writers.

# Also by Edward Turner

Ghosts of Paris: Ten Haunted Places in the City of Love
Appalachian Nightmares: The Top 10 Creepy Creatures of the Mountains
Asia's Top Ten Cryptids: Legends, Sightings, and Theories
Beyond the Shadows: Unlocking the Mystery of Bigfoot
Evil Women in History: Uncovering the Gruesome Crimes of Ten Notorious Female Killers
Ghosts of London: Ten Haunted Places in The City
Ghosts of New York: Ten Haunted Places in The Big Apple
Ghosts of Oregon: The Top 10 Haunted Places You Must Visit
Missouri Nightmares: The Top 10 Chilling Legends
Mothman Unleashed: Into the Darkened Skies
North America's Top Ten Cryptids: Legends, Sightings, and Theories
Philly's Phantom Encounters: Exploring the City's Most Haunted Places
Secrets of the Deep: The Mystery of the Loch Ness Monster
Unsolved Mysteries: Delving into the Shadows of Infamous Murders and Enigmatic Killers
Unveiling the Shadows: A Journey into Financial Crimes and Scandals

# About the Author

Edward Turner is a renowned author who specializes in exploring the realms of ghosts, the paranormal, and cryptids. With a captivating writing style and an insatiable curiosity for the unknown, Turner has garnered a dedicated following of readers who are captivated by his thrilling and eerie tales.

Born with an innate fascination for the supernatural, Turner has spent decades delving into the depths of paranormal phenomena, unearthing captivating stories and untangling mysteries that lie beyond the veil of the ordinary. His extensive research and meticulous attention to detail have earned him a reputation as a leading authority in the field.

Through his books, Turner expertly weaves together chilling accounts of encounters with ghosts, offering readers a glimpse into the ethereal world that coexists alongside our own. His ability to paint vivid portraits of spectral apparitions and convey the haunting atmosphere of haunted locations has made his works both spine-tingling and thought-provoking.

Turner's exploration of the paranormal doesn't stop at ghosts. He also dives into the fascinating world of cryptids—creatures that defy conventional explanation. His in-depth investigations into legendary creatures such as Bigfoot, the Loch Ness Monster, and the Chupacabra showcase his commitment to shedding light on these enigmatic beings.

With each page, Edward Turner's readers are drawn deeper into the enigmatic and unknown. His unique storytelling ability combined with his meticulous research has made him a sought-after author for those with an insatiable thirst for the supernatural. Whether delving into ghostly encounters or unraveling the mysteries of elusive cryptids, Turner's books offer a spine-chilling and immersive reading experience that leaves readers questioning the boundaries of our reality.

Edward Turner's works have earned critical acclaim and numerous accolades within the paranormal genre. He continues to explore the unexplained, captivating readers with his distinctive narrative style and unwavering dedication to unveiling the mysteries that lie hidden in the shadows.